THE NEW WORLD

POETRY BOOKS BY TOM CLARK

Airplanes (Once, 1966)
The Sand Burg (Ferry, 1966)
Bun (with Ron Padgett) (Angel Hair, 1968)
Stones (Harper & Row, 1969)
Chicago (with Lewis Warsh) (Angel Hair, 1969)
Air (Harper & Row, 1970)
Green (Black Sparrow, 1971)
Neil Young (Coach House, 1971)
John's Heart (Goliard/Grossman, 1972)
Smack (Black Sparrow, 1972)
Blue (Black Sparrow, 1974)
At Malibu (Kulchur, 1975)
35 (Poltroon 1976)
Fan Poems (North Atlantic, 1976)
How I Broke In (Tombouctou, 1977)
The Mutabilitie of the Englishe Lyrick (Poltroon, 1978)
When Things Get Tough on Easy Street: Selected Poems 1963-1978
        (Black Sparrow, 1978)
The End of the Line (Little Caesar, 1980)
A Short Guide to the High Plains (Cadmus, 1981)
Nine Songs (Turkey, 1981)
Under the Fortune Palms (Turkey, 1982)
Paradise Resisted: Selected Poems *1978-1984* (Black Sparrow, 1984)
Property (Illuminati, 1984)
The Border (Coffee House, 1985)
Disordered Ideas (Black Sparrow, 1987)
Apocalyptic Talkshow (Bloody Twin, 1987)
His Supposition (Werkman, 1987)
Easter Sunday (Coffee House, 1988)
Fractured Karma (Black Sparrow, 1990)
Sleepwalker's Fate: New and Selected Poems 1965-1991 (Black Sparrow, 1992)
Junkets on a Sad Planet: Scenes from the Life of John Keats (Black Sparrow, 1994)
Like Real People (Black Sparrow, 1995)
Empire of Skin (Black Sparrow, 1997)
White Thought (Hard Press/The Figures, 1997)
Cold Spring: A Diary (Skanky Possum, 2000)
Zombie Dawn (with Anne Waldman) (Skanky Possum, 2003)
Night Sky (Deep Forest, 2004)
Threnody (Effing, 2006)
Light and Shade: New and Selected Poems (Coffee House, 2006)

Tom Clark

THE NEW WORLD

Libellum
2009

Some of these poems first appeared in *The American Poetry Review, The Argotist (U.K.), Best American Poetry* blog, *Big Bridge, Coconut, Exquisite Corpse, House Organ, Jacket, The Kenyon Review, Other Stuff* blog, *Tom Clark/ Beyond the Pale* blog, *Vanitas* blog.

The italicized lines in "What Can I Say" are from a comment posted on Tom Clark's blog by a pseudonymous blogger from Tehran who calls herself *human being.*

Cover photograph: Tom and Angelica Clark, 2009, copyright by Juliet Clark
Photograph on page 8: Tom, Angelica and Juliet Clark, 1973, copyright by Gerard Malanga
Graphic Coordination: Juan Gomez

First Edition

Libellum 7

Libellum
211 West 19th Street, #5
New York, NY 10011
libellum@mac.com

Distributed by Small Press Distribution
www.spdbooks.org telephone 510-524-1668
and
Fotofolio
www.fotofolio.com telephone 212-226-0923

ISBN 0-9752993-7-9

Table Of Contents

A Retrospect

1   *A Retrospect*   1798/2008

Time's arrow, Orfeo, never turns around,
So don't look back.   *Rocks and stones hurled round*
In their diurnal course were all I saw go past
For a while, but before that, somewhere pleasant
With greenery and water, sweet, I'd go back
In a minute, just to look, had I chance,
How fine things were in the morning of the world,
Said the jumper from the tall building, halfway down,
To himself.   *You must change your life.*   Then he woke
Into the cold dark morning that *is*,
Shocked by the familiar impact
Of reality, that joke that is always
On the one who attempts to tell it,
Once more having failed to change his life.

2 *To a Ghost*   1798/2008

I wrote and wrote, the candle light flickering
Upon the cottage wall, the smoldering fire
Fuming like someone in a not great mood,
Burning damp wood throughout the eco-slump.
A ghost kept coming and going, flitting
In and out of the woodwork of the poem
Through the holes chewed by Will, Sam and Charles
The three blind mice in my morality
Play, whose hero, a dark stranger Shelley,
Turned a whiter shade of pale revealing
He had never been really real
Alackaday!   I'd thought a phantasm was
Charles Lamb or Samuel Taylor Coleridge,
The gated community of my mind
Nether Stowey or London or the Lakes
In 1798! The pure and simple
Wishful thinking of a perfect old fool
O Stranger!   You existed in my hopeful
Imagination only. When will I learn?
There you were, daft thought, but then you weren't.
I made you up, Mister Lonely, going
Out the door of the poem before
Ever coming into the picture
With any clarity — for *clear*'s not you,
As I've just learnt, vague memory person.

3 *Lost at Midnight* 1798/2008

And then a different kind of friend appears
From intimate historical woodwork, chased
By mice out into the open of this closed
Off little world. No more beautiful
Than good, for all the good it's done you,
Or all the worth of being either
In an oh so old and timewarped world
But is this in fact an either/or
And really, when you get down to it,
Isn't the good more or less identical
With the beautiful? The thumping you hear
Is the footfall of Beauty as she goes
Her morning rounds. A sound may be a picture
Of reality as we imagine it,
Or should I say desire it, dear.
And then, blink, we are our grandparents
Physically, yet estranged in our minds
From all but *this*, *now*. North wind, power goes out,
A candle's lit creating shadow play.
Click *Memory*, unwanted, unexpected
Images *Display;* pasts come flooding in, slow,
Flicking yellow glow on endarkened wall. Hello
Interior landscape we've always
Traveled, Dear One, by a Lake of Dreams — looking
For that light-in-window fleeting house
Now a cottage haunted by passing strangers
Who were never there. The night's cold,
Bells do not toll here at midnight any more.

4 *Flash Player* 2008

Strange to turn to old ghosts, watch ourselves dissolve
In their eyes. They were not here to help us,
Merely to drag us back against our will
Into a dim becalmed past, then forward into
Occluded presents which yet *feel too bright.*

5 *Click* 2008/2046/2666

One may age ten years in ten minutes.
It's too quiet. I can hear the crickets,
It's like a music of the spheres in reverse,
A whack recursiveness of thinking,
Or is it just the night-clicking computer god
And what kind of iterative god is that?

Pascal had his pit, which went with him
Where'er he went, like a faithful dog,
Nor was he out of it. Infinity I can see
From here. It looks empty, unrelenting,
Cold. There is no respite from Being
And Number, a poet once told us that

When it was getting late for him
And night panic passed through his hair
Making it stand on end, the little he still
Had of it. I'll go to the wall, stand with it,
Let it be my friend, just to have something
That won't fall down. I feel giddy, said the clown.

I believe in a world. Is God or death more great?
This world is my world and will vanish with me
But while I *click* it goes on existing
In eternity — to 2046 or
2666, or whene'er the chips melt down.
I've lost *Memory* writing this.

I've aged ridiculously in ten minutes,

Maybe ten years. Distance is closing in,
It's too quiet. I can hear the crickets
Singing God and death out of existence.
More power to them. *Click*.
The intricate circuits of a summer night.

6 *Light and Shade* 2008

Is it ocean sound or wind in the big dark trees
Or is it simply time passing in my mind
And not crickets but car tires hissing by?
Days, nights full of spectres.   Light and shade
No longer so easy to keep apart, the dark
Parts invading the bright parts making gray
This moment, always just a moment away
From that moment, the moments bleeding
Into one another until at last they stop.

7 *Slide Area*   New Years Eve 1969

One dreams up metaphors — bright light,
Deep shade, shifting animal information
Patterns coalescing, changing, thoughts too swift
To "read," if intelligible at all
Then only as curious complication
Felt and *lived*.   Kaleidoscopic window
Mosaic of colored glass and agates
We all gathered at that windswept beach
Through which blurred images of melting faces
Loom up, reflective of self or other as
Vague ghosts of poets past are put to rest,
Later we're all strung out on the cold beach,
Nightwaves pounding, whitecaps collapsing
In foam-swirl upon driftwood littered
Strand, neath trillion starred black heavens,
Time passing, the undercurrent then turning
Back toward China, all eyes drawn to the vast
Infinite sky, its deep blue dome concealing
All the pain to descend over coming years —
Forgetting now washed over all that, all this —
Ocean Parkway, slide-reft, no longer exists.

8 *The Fault at the End of Time*   2008/1968

Keep returning in my mind as to a Pole
To that lost idea of a paradise
Located in a long ago Bolinas,
O Ghost, as we remember it thus.
Time passing in foggy places is slow,
The senses recall woodsmoke, eucalyptus
Odor acrid on the air, frogs singing
Though no more were *those the days* than this is;
And, speaking, one nonetheless thinks it's
Not language we'll need to escape this crisis —
No one's talking about getting out alive —
Too late to flee, as if escape existed,
To any of one's paradises lost. Try
Bolinas a belated Lake District
Circa 1968 for instance
One designates *this* as it was then in one's mind —
This place of water and sweet greenery
This fault in space at the end of time,
A place separated from America
As in the beginning paradise
Was separated from humankind
By a fault — and so it was apes became
Separated from paradise — in paradise
Every thing has its own sign, so that
There was no need for language, in paradise
One could converse with herons and with pines
Without need for other kinds of signs
But all of this was happening on the other
The other side the other side of the fault

Line that separated humankind from
Paradise and paradise from humankind
And so too then in the end it was by
A fault that we were separated
From that paradise.

Nasturtiums and Eucalypti (for Philip Whalen)

The plum-lacquered woven Japanese basket Phil
Lately back from Kyoto gave us,
Juliet's baby bed on Nymph and Cherry,
The year Phil dwelt over on Larch with Don A.
Beyond the shimmering silver dollar eucalypti,
Still packed away in the basement to this day.

Sometimes strolled two dirt road blocks to visit.
People mad at him if he came over, or if he didn't,
He averred.   Even in paradise poverty is a bother.
Tones if not words are always recollected.
Portly Bodhidharma mendicant
Toting his laundry downtown, two sad sacks.

Later on he camped down on Terrace tender
Dear heart crotchety and all alone as a song
In the same town with his vivacious Muse,
The elusive butterfly diva, Joanne K.,
Not quite on the outs and not quite on the ins with her,
Impatient amid nasturtiums as the day was long.

Time fills in the holes, cement in the ocean,
Dark parts of memory shading into bright.
One day when on acid the eucalyptus tilted,
A circus of silliness shimmering into play,
Phil sternly informed me, Thomas Clark,
Poetry will never get written this way.

After the Squall (for Robert Duncan)

How the arm moved
Throwing the poet's

Ashes out of the boat
How it all comes back

To where it started
How the whole story

Form of telling curves
The story around

Impossible corners
How brief lives

Have eternity
Inscribed

In recursive
Character

How the stars swam
How the moon

Was dying down
Out over the water

To loosen out into
Those big quiet waters

Little pieces of
The whole story

Are floating on
After the squall

Fidelity

Fidelity, after long practice, to
The things that have crossed one's path in life,
Moves one to find "history" in a morning,
A moonlit night, a transitory patch
Of sun upon grass, the turning of a cat's
Sleek head over its shoulder to look back
Into one's eyes, a lifelong lover's touch,
The memory of the shy sweet sidelong
Smile of a friend one may not see again
In "this life" — these things define *home*
To one now that one lives largely in one's mind —
As though there had ever been any other
Place — once born, once having existed —
In which to somehow locate a world

Because brief hours before fadeout life becomes
A late awakening, much as one assumes
Is the experience of "lost" generations
Whose youth is turned back toward childhood by
Dreams; just so one's own dim youth now at last
Appears a kind of slumber from which the slow
Process of waking took a half century
Or so, as time now opens up its eyes,
Yawns, stretches, struggles in dark to discover
Where it is among whirling things, places, years.
But of course one will never fully emerge
From this fog, nor in one's heart wish to do so,
For mere excursions don't suffice on visits

To dead cities — excavation too's required,
Cries out the hungry unborn poem
Within us, demanding to exist *as*
If alive

Persistence of Memory

I think he's saying it's quite easily caught.
I'm not hearing as well as once I was.
Did he say the yen is advancing against
The flower? What flower? A yen for what
Was that again?   Starting to forget things
Changes one's mind. The not remembering
Is not so bad, it's the resurgences of not
Forgetting that ruin everything. Yesterday's
Papers landing at the door with a soft
Lamenting thud, though one had not subscribed,
The shouting silence of the midnight hour,
The soft footfalls of the ocelot through the house.

For Delmore Schwartz

The night they caught you, I dreamt you sank
Through oozy blooms to lean against a coral tree
Cornered by nebulous cop-fates escaped from ghost tv
On the dime of moonlight where they spidered down
A ladder from the hovering chopper to net you, wan
Beams lighting up a chalky face devoid of color
As some old clown's beginning to make up before a show,
Bright bars playing variations about the bone
Mimicking out-of-focus body scans that give
Too little definition between the known shadow
And the shadow of the actual unknown
From which you always stole away like a fugitive.

Clean

Oft turns the ageing mind to Frances
Waldman's blunt query, back seat of full taxi,
Riding downtown, that chill February,
To young Angelica: "*Maybe marrying*
Him seems like a good idea now, but where
Will it leave you in forty years?" Being there
Herself, she should have known: old. Low blow, Frances!
The minds of the old are dirty, dirty
With the pained truth of all those years. Old, one grows,
At least in the opinion of strangers,
Ever less loveable (fact of nature), and so,
It follows, ever less easily loved —
Yet still, old does not so easily
Surrender the capacity to love
Nor the need to be loved. If anything
These things increase as one ages, somewhat
Inconveniently let it be said.
No one young likes to think of love among
The old. Consider the film *Cloud Nine*
In which seventy-somethings conduct
A none-too-discreet affair: things get sloppy,
No fleshy detail's spared us. Would you
O reader, not yet superannuated,
Wish to look away? En route to dust, let us
Guard and preserve, if not our virginity
(*Pace* Andrew Marvell), then our privacy.
Let's not talk about dignity, only wild
Creatures get to maintain that. And of course
As I'm writing this, Smokey the cat

Fastidiously scours his private parts with
Busy tongue. Animals, unlike us, are clean.
Young, the parts that interested one
Most in books and movies were the dirty ones.

Born Yesterday

The concept of evil, as long ago
Symbolized by the devil, has evolved
Over centuries into the concept
Of *men*, as delineated by (let's
Call her) Naima, Halloween night
At Fertile Grounds, where she stood
Demurely chatting with Ayman, the handsome
Proprietor (think Omar Sharif
With soul and twinkle) at closing time,
As I poked my ancient nose in and said
"Trick or treat."   Ayman offered a knuckle
Bump solidarity hello — alone there
By the counter with lovely young Naima,
Who, when I said, What's new, smiled
Ever so sweetly and said, "Men are evil!"
Feeling it ungracious to disagree
I didn't, for a moment.   But then —
Well, solidarity is solidarity.
"What about Ayman?" I said.   "Ayman
Doesn't look evil to me."   Naima
Fixed upon Ayman a glance of great
Critical probity, smiled and said, "Hmm,"
A moment passed, pregnant, perhaps
With reconsideration.   Exceptions
Prove rules are basically dumb,
And really, that's the trouble, after all,
With generalization.   And what of love?
"Isn't love," I ventured, "a matter of
Recognizing someone has flaws

And trying to help them limit the damage?"
More thought. "Yes, that's exactly what it is,"
Naima said. And to myself I said,
One point for a draw, quit while you're not losing.
I fell out the door, squeezing between raindrops.
Two ten-year-old girls walked past, one with horns,
The other peeping from a full body cast.
You forgot your treat, Ayman called out,
Holding up a bag of old pastries
From the "Born Yesterday" basket.

A Meditation Outside the Fertile Grounds Cafe

Ayman just came back from his family
Home in the West Bank. How's the spirit there?
I asked. "Good. Nobody's giving up."
Ayman paused, wiping down the spotless glass top
Of the pastry case one more careful time
Without looking up. Thinking to himself.
"After all, all they want's a little justice."
On the map of the West Bank, that blank space
Just to the left of the town of Bhiddu
Is the village where Ayman's father, one
Of twenty children, was born and raised.
The name of the village means House of Stones
"Because there's a quarry there," but still
It's too small to rate a spot on the map in
The Economist, alongside this story
On the fresh welling up of blood and anger
In my friend's home land, that blank space
Filled with blood and stones. Ayman loves
His trade; in six years he's built from nothing
The coolest little coffee shop on the street;
People like him, he likes them; he makes
Great coffee, his sandwiches are famed, justly;
It's the old American Horatio
Alger Dream, and America's his country.
Every day he gets hundreds of calls
On his cell phone. "But know how many
Calls from people here I take when I'm back
Home?" he smiles. "None. I talk to people
There." And when he goes back home to Beit

Duqqu, America feels far away.
That's the way it feels to me too, but I have
No other home. The photo of the olive tree,
Its roots exposed from the bulldozer cut,
That was up on Ayman's wall last autumn —
Is that a photo of a *broken home*
Or is it that one's home's always intact
In one's mind as long as one's heart is
Full? I wouldn't begin to know. Tacked
On a phone pole out front of Fertile Grounds
In drifting night mist, a tattered poster
With a picture of a cat's face on it, lost
Near Delaware and Shattuck. It's Momo.
And what's become of poor Momo, now a week
Gone? Tonight, caning into the fog,
I hallucinated a Momo
Sighting downtown. No, just another feral.
Over ferals few sentimental
Tears are shed. A shelter's not a home.
A sanctuary's what everybody needs
These days — the ferals, the street and doorway
People, the drifters in the mist, the bums.
On my way back, as I passed, I saw that
A young Arab girl in headscarf sat weeping
At a table outside Fertile Grounds. Ayman
In his counterman's apron, spick and span,
And Mohamed stood huddled in conference,
Mo holding a cell phone. "She's just lost
Her family, everything," Mo said softly.

"She doesn't have people here. I am
Going to help her." Ayman was talking
To the girl in Arabic, serious, hushed.
Then too Mo, in Arabic, reassuring.
"Don't worry, it will be okay," said Mo —
Switching back to Shattuck Avenue English
For me, the infidel. God is great. May
God bring Momo home if it is His will,
And everybody else along with him,
Whomever that may include — we, living —
And we'll abide in that, and till then hope
That Momo too, pilfering out of the trash
Bins behind the Shattuck eateries,
Will abide likewise. He'll not lack competition.

Lost

Even on the mean concrete streets
Of Berkeley there are lost deer at night
This time of year, run off the hills, descending
To look for water and, not finding it,
Settling for nibbling the leaves of rose
And other bushes in people's back yards

Last fall this time, standing in the daytime rush
Hour street out front, now vacant this once
Because it was peaceful three in the morning
I heard familiar light tap dancer steps
On pavement that alerted me to
A presence I knew could not be another

Clumsy human like me, turned and saw close by,
Surprised as I was by our chance meeting,
Ears cocked toward me and likewise frozen,
A big deer, calculating whether to make
A run for safety yet no doubt in the same
Moment aware in cities there's no safety

For deer — we stood both thus transfixed,
Till I looked away, knowing in this turning
I would allow our night encounter to end —
As so it did, for in those seconds more
Light footsteps told me the visitor was
Moving away up into darkness toward...?

Toribio

Christmas Eve of the New Depression year
And as usual Toribio's at his station
In the doorway of the French Hotel café
Philosophical, diffident, unhurried
Among his *compadres*, exchanging words
Now and then with tonight's counter man
Jesus, the *joven* whose brother-in-law
Cecilio even now tends counter three
Blocks south at Fertile Grounds — the useful
Underground railroad of coffee servers
Floor moppers and sink and basin scrubbers,
Without whom no necessary caffeine jolt
Of temporary cognitive enhancement
To keep anxious Christmas shoppers bent
To last minute buying rounds — the street's high end
Food markets overrun now by busy crowds
Of cautiously intent-on-consuming
Festive season celebrants; Toribio
However half skeptical looks upon
It all and comments bargain sales are good
Business this year, this is good for
Everybody.   Is Toribio
Serious?   I can't make this out, then later
Chastise myself for doubting, and tell
Toribio so.   He nods understanding
It's my fate accorded me by my name
That of the doubting Saint who insisted
On sticking a dubious finger in the wound
In the side of Jesus — the earlier one

I mean, the one born in Bethlehem,
So long ago. Toribio is thirty
Three, same age at which the original
Jesus died, as I once suggested
While he stood on a Saturday night watching
The fancy *muchachas* prance up Shattuck past
The French — slouched against the bricks, checking
Out the beauteous *piernas largas*
And sipping an Anchor Steam from a brown
Paper bag. When Toribio washes
Dishes across the street some nights a week
The money he makes he sets aside,
Eats lightly, rides a bike, lets time go by
And on the weekend buys two twenty-
Fours of Anchor and goes through one per
Night, his humor minimally improved,
His philosophy deepened, his mood made
More serene yet his nocturnal routine
Unaltered, and on one such night I
Bring up his age conjunction with Jesus
And ask him, doubting, Toribio do you
Think Jesus had a good time?   Of course he did
Says Toribio, he had life didn't he?
And if there were Anchor Steam, Toribio,
In Jesus' time, would that have made his life good?
Somber Toribio nods, *por supuesto.*

Toribio has no family here yet does,
Toribio will spend Christmas with friends

Toribio's Christmas present to himself
— He's already told me, and when he did
I made a pretend fist, chucked his wind
Breakered shoulder and said *Que hombre,*
Muy fuerte, with sincerity — will be ten
Twenty-fours, which he will make grace with joy
The ten days of his migrant's Christmas.

In Toribio there is some Vasquez
Family blood from back in Jalisco
And some Gonzalez, and the Gonzalez
Blood connects Toribio with his namesake
Santo Toribio Romo Gonzalez
The *Santo Pollero* or Holy Illegal
Alien Smuggler — a Saint, canonized
In Dos Mil by Papa Paulo Dos. All this
I learned one cold full moon night in November,
It was a Saturday night, the pretty young
Woman who cleans the rooms was dancing
And singing — a good feeling in the air —
She insisted the moon was not quite full,
Toribio's bantamweight-sized *hermano*
Lucho the Antonio Margarito
Fan insisted good natured *la luna esta*
Llena: when I tilted my head I could see both
Points of view and said so, and at that moment

Toribio said Santo Toribio
Is here. *Quien* I said? Santo Toribio,
He said, he is alive, he is here. I looked around.
Traffic was rolling up the street. The moon
Sat upon the tops of a few scant bare branches

Above the post office.   He is everywhere,
Said Toribio.   He comes when you need him.
I now know he spoke then of his ancestor
And namesake, the patron saint of the needy
Migratores, who appears in the night
To help them get across the river, provides
Food and water at the other side, soothes
Fevered brows in the desert crossing, heals
Snake bite.   I felt a chill in my spine
As Toribio first explained all this that
Full moon night, a ghost story about a Scarlet
Pimpernel priest dead these eighty years,
Killed by *federales* in his sleep, in
Santa Ana, near Jalostotitlan,
Jalisco.   If you need him he will come.
He is here, he is there, he is everywhere.

As the nights went by and times got harder
And nights got colder, I more than once quizzed
Toribio as to when the Saint
Might be expected to show up, given
The evident ambient state of need
On this street of illegals and bodies
Huddled in doorways more numerous
Each night.   Toribio sneered
As though I had no idea of the true meaning
Of need.   *Que, no lo necessitamos?*
Toribio shook his head.   If saints
Had to come every time you need them
There would have to be many saints, *muchos*
Santos not just one, Toribio said.

All Saints (Shattuck Avenue, Early New Depression)

6.432   How *things are in the world is a matter of complete indifference for what is higher.   God does not reveal himself in the world.*
6.4321 *The facts all contribute only to setting the problem, not to its solution.*
6.44   *It is not how things are in the world that is mystical, but that it exists.*
6.45   *To view the world* sub specie aeterni *is to view it as a whole — a limited whole.*

     Feeling the world as a whole — it is this that is mystical.

          — Wittgenstein, *Tractatus Logico-Philosophicus*

*

a'bject.   *A man without hope; a man whose miseries are irretrievable.*

    But in mine adversity they rejoiced, and gathered themselves together; yea, the abjects gathered themselves together against me, and I knew it not.
    They did tear me, and ceased not.   Psalms XXX, 15.

        — Johnson's *Dictionary*

*

I've found all saints lost at midnight in the rain
Seek shop doorways fit to lay their bodies down
And dwell upon the sins that have expelled them:
Those sins, O Friend, which they perceive as wounds

Inflicted they know neither why nor by whom,
Nor in defiance of what remorseless laws.
The wind that rakes the street is unforgiving,
Warmth but a memory, winter coming on,

The concrete cold, the cardboard pallet sodden,
God far away, but unfortunately not Man,
Who motors past to get to bars or home,
Completely unaware they're bedding there,

Splashing sheets of grey water out of puddles
That wash over them in chill waves they may
If they so choose trust to wash their sins away,
Dimly aware at last they're given something.

Haunted (Halloween Week '08)

Schlepping for eats *sans* cash check credit card out
Pop the convenience store demon pumpkin
Ghost reminders to *one* a long year now jobless
Involuntarily and unwillingly
Embarrassed — *one's* "company" these nights the "street
People" half warily accepting *one* as
"One of their own" — forlorn haunted nation
Of the streets, *one* and *one* and *one* and *one*

And *one* in a demography of monads —
Or demons, depending on your point of view —
A caste changing with the economy (bad)
And the weather (mixed) from half-assed half-witted
Rejects of the better groomed classes
Who step over them as they politely beg
On the block anchored by the money bags
Of Chez Panisse, to true untouchables —

As has happened these past months, weeks —
"They think they better *than other people"*
Quoth Sharon the sweet frizzy haired "three stroke"
Shattuck and Cedar beggar lady, late, hard
Put to reach her required fifty dollar
Nightly begging take — Sighing, looking a bit
Careworn despite her sweet smile, earnest
Lipstick and makeup — Sharon's *known*, Sharon loves

One, loves everyone — *"The Good Lord don't put*
On you nothing you can't take" — more exiting

Diners clutching big purses and bulging
Doggy bags stroll past ignoring her
Sad tired rehearsed entreaties, unregarding
Trying to appear not to notice yet not
Quite able to conceal the anxious corner-
Of-the-eye glance that distances them from

Her (and friend *one*) as *one* very bright solar
System is distanced from *any* black hole
The quantum physics of social class working
Itself out on the city streets — and as
If lit up in *Scream* horror neon overhead
Appears to me that line of Seferis
About life under an earlier fascism
Lord don't let me die among these people

The People

The people of the street possess a weird freedom
From the fading vestiges of the American Dream,
That straitjacket worn much as the suit of armor
Of the knight who, glimpsing his reflection, pitched
Headfirst into the moat and was not again seen,
Dragged under by the weight of his own protection
From what in the end he would never even know.
Self knowledge being the last property to come,
The first to go. Another cold night, body pain, slow
Progress between Vine and Safeway, paused at
The corner hailed by Dave the Irishman, now shorn
Of his beloved and badly abused canine companion
Jezebel, sequestered in the pound
For the nth time a month ago, ne'er to return
As Dave could not pay the fee this time round.
Dave is banned on Shattuck.   Clustered up
With the tall haunted Tom Waits lookalike guy
And a Latin dude with a handheld video player,
Carrying a formidable knife.   Dave proffered
A Foster's in a paper bag, the invisibilizing
Container which shields crime from police eyes.
The night deepened.   Some drunken high school
Kids mocked us from the bus stop, falling over.
Unconcerned, Dave cartwheeled round the corner.
A couple of gangsters sidled past casting
Meaningful glances at the video player
And the Latin dude's hand moved to the pocket
With the knife. At the stoplight a well dressed
Couple stepping carefully around us, compressing

The distance between their four hundred
Dollar Chez Panisse dinner and their parked
Ride to as few tiny cautious steps as possible,
Not saying a word, stiff with body armament,
And then traffic flowed with the changing of the light.

Fireside Chat

You really think free advice is worth money?
An old ghost rising up clammier than ever,
You can hear his teeth rattling. Let's call
Him Fear Itself, and nestle up closer
To the warm and fatherly radio
Whence issue deep and reassuring words.
At the other end of the transmission
A world of static and black-edged clouds away
You can hear the fire crackling in the hearth
And if you strain your ears you might make out
A distant barking, perhaps the voice of Falla,
Woolly anachronism from a lost epoch.
Dogs speak in unintelligible words. Arf!
I take that back: unintelligible
To *us*. And we're not reassured. Crisis
Of confidence time, then: credit default
Occurs when you can't buy what they're saying.
But wait, did you ever? Bought situation
City all these years and now someone's
Surprised? Do crocodiles cry rivers
In order to have someplace to swim? Time for
Regulation arrives at one minute
Before the sun yo-yos up into the sky
And that tinny barking starts up again. Woof!
High time to begin drawing limits to thought.
This may be a fight for life. We may find
Both sides of the limit unthinkable. We may
Have to be able to think what can't be thought,
Credit crunch or no. *Credo* means I believe

In crop circles. Or did I mean church
May be the last sanctuary of deceived
Believers in the free market dream?
You'll find a crescent-shaped scar on my wrist
To prove to you this was no mere nightmare.
I'm in a weakened condition so go easy.
What can I do but hand over the payroll?

Lines Not Written Wearing Mouse Ears

"I'd be burned out too.   Disneyland
Is awesome but it's tiring."   I guess I'd hoped
Despite myself the Cal student slouching
Down Shattuck gassing on cell with his
Girlfriend (?) would be addressing the *world
Going on*, which they'll have to live in
After Tuesday.   But maybe they're Young
Republicans; I never have a clue
Any more.   I was down with the New
Frontier.   Senior year wore my hair
Like Kennedy's.   Had never imitated
Ike's hairdo, skinheads weren't in, then.
Crusade in Europe however made
My Top 5 Books Read in the Forties
List, tied for fifth with *Blood, Sweat and Tears*.
One through four: *Navy Blue and Gold, Seventeenth
Summer, The Kid from Left Field, The Seven
Wonders of the World*.   I too dug *Ghost Riders
In the Sky*, though to my priest-trained ears it rang
With vivid personal Apocalypse
Associations.   At that time the Four
Horsemen of Notre Dame were still famous
In my Chicago Irish neighborhood and
In my mind; I could tell you their names today
And would, were there not *a world going on*.
Indeed I had an envied grade school chum,
Ed Collins, whose dad had been one of
The Seven Mules; that, to me, was buzzworthy.
Have you ever seen that film, *The Rapture?*   She goes

Out in the wilderness to receive the light.
But it doesn't come. Just cops. Later arrive
The Apocalypse horses, however, and
Bust down the jailhouse walls. You'll recall
Joshua's chart-topping ditty at
Jericho — down tumble the bricks. We've *fit*
This battle before, to what end? But then, *it's*
All good, you feel me? End times can resemble
Starts (*We've only just begun*, as Karen C.,
Starving to death amid the fat of the land,
Once warbled in that bank commercial)
To fools like us. It's like in *The Master*
And Margarita, in the Russian TV
Movie version, where Pontius Pilate
And Jesus walk off into the stars: *He walks*
With me, He talks with me, He calls me his own
As the long day closes. Now it's deep night, rain,
I'm scribbling this with a borrowed pen, huddling
Beneath an arcade for shelter
In a public place, as occasional grey
Incurious strangers — lost souls like me? —
Drift past. One nation, indivisible
Or was it invisible? mere hours before
The polls open. Annette Funicello
I liked in seventh grade, but mouse ears
I never wore, O Friend! My top three
Songs of the pre-Korean War epoch
Were *Rum and Coca-Cola, Perfidia,*
Hernando's Hideaway; honorable

Mention goes to that one about *standing*
On a corner by a pawnshop in Pittsburgh,
Pennsylvania, watching all the girls
Go by. So, *Where were the girls?* They were going
By that corner. I remember that song
Swamping my pre-adolescent psyche
Through an entire Cub Scout den meeting
At Billy Beaver's house. Billy had a weight
Problem; was good at tying knots, but on
Our frontiering expedition to the wild
Scrub margins of the West Side — this before
The suburbs extended all the way west
To Iowa — managed to fall off a branch-bridge
Over the world's puniest creek. Wet buns
For Billy's campfire hot dogs, that sad day.
And *where were the girls* then, were they camping
Happily by their own fireside along
The Allegheny, the Monongahela
Or the Ohio, laughing at us? Before
Men are evil, one fears, boys are silly.
Is That All There Is? Peggy Lee sounded
Justifiably disappointed. *Fever*
Kindled in me such heats that, after hearing
It in the back of a convertible en
Route to a softball game in La Grange, or some
Such western outpost, my suppressed and
Unacknowledged passion for unsuspecting
Fourteen-year-old Jan D. so distracted
Me that, playing first base, I lost a popup
In the lights, dropped it, and still wince almost
As painfully at the memory as when
The event happened. But where was I?

Somewhere around 1954?   From the subsequent
Early-adolescent period, *Ebb
Tide, Stranger in Paradise, Volare*
Probably topped my private charts.   This was
Mid-America, remember; little
Freedom to choose, definitely no
Alan Freed to guide one.   But to get back to your
Question, burning like a plutonium
Ingot in the pants of an action hero,
Where were the girls?   Dipping *Volare*
In my cut-price Proustian teacup, I get
Faint echoes of that then popular tune
Being played by the Chicago Cubs'
Ballpark organist.   I had an ushering job
As well as a crush on a girl from Wheaton
I'd met there at Wrigley, dusting off her box
Seat before a game.   She spilled popcorn
On the lap of her madras bermudas;
Trained by the book to be heroic
In my blue-and-gold uniform, I stepped
Into the breach and offered to help her
Clean things up down there.   Immense surprise!
She declined, and not even all that
Gratefully.   Girls see things another way,
There was no choice but to then conclude.
I rued my foolish move all the way home
On the Chicago & Northwestern.   What did
I know of girls' tragic magic, then?
Or of my *own* motives, for that matter?   Then
There came a quickening of the tempo:
Sh'Boom, Shake, Rattle & Roll.   Something like
Apprehension began to dawn: *Earth Angel,*

Heard on a transistor in the basketball
Team bus, signalled an upheaval of sorts.   Next
Occurred The Awakening: *Kathy's
Clown* — *where were the girls* I imagined
Clustering around Don and Phil?   Gone,
If one was to believe the song.   And then in time,
Peggy Sue — I loved that stutter of Buddy's,
Signature, as I thought, of an existential
Urgency I understood; few songs could have
Gladdened me more than it did when, wind blowing
In our hair through the windows of my Olds,
I drove *the girls* to beaches by the Great
Lakes of my first real adventures
In biology with the opposite sex.
And in the dark western woods beyond
The city lights, there was that p arking spot
Called *Tail Light*, because cops, stopping in on
Their rounds to peep into steamed-up car
Windows o'winter nights, never interfered
As long as you kept your tail-lights on.   Red
Evidence of a rich interior life
Wasted on impressionable children
Of the benighted prairie, as seen from
The eyes of voyeurs with badges.   O Friend!
Did you ever hear Zappa's song *Catholic
Girls?* The phenomena Frank attested
Were less local-regional than ethnic-
Cultural, one suspects, as prevalent
In Chicago as in New York or Rome.
Catholic girls were like Disneyland,
Awesome.   Had I had strength to brave that
Daunting conflagration — think, if you will, O

Friend, of the lava storms of Mt. St. Helens;
Or better still, of Vesuvius, youthful me
Stranded in Pompeii, my toga wrapped
Ineffectually about my feeble
Loins to protect me from the fires
To come — I'd be *burned out* too, by now.
But though that boiling crater's long since
Banked its flames and cooled for good, still it's true:
There's a world going on, and I'm stuck in it;
The girls are old too; now we're *all* in it —
Whatever it is, this weird world — together.

The New World

Eruptions of starlight, joy and gladness
As, at 10:30 p.m. on Shattuck, the New
World dawns with shouts of *"Yes we can!"*
From young persons thronging the clogged street.
The street people, however, are just trying
To get some sleep. I infer this from the body-
Bundles I see huddled in every alcove. But why,
In the rapture of intoxicated victory
I glimpse around me, do I insist on this
Dissonant note? *"A complete curmudgeon,"*
Gentle Dorothy once called me, in
Exasperation, accurately,
I cannot deny. Aye, O Friend! I fear there are
What are lately called Depression Issues
At work here. How tiresome, really.
By Depression do I mean the mental kind
And am I signalling I "need help"? Some,
I'm told, might well secretly think so.
"And maybe they're right, William," tenders
Gentle Dorothy from across the hearthside.
The nights are growing sharp, November
In the Cumberlands, ancient aching joints,
Getting up in the dark and seeing your breath,
Bad patches of thatch to fix before frost
Closes in and fingers, too numb for labors,
Withdrawn into religious half-mittens.

There were street people in William's village
Too. But in knowable communities

That which is often seen soon becomes known,
Thus accepted and not stepped over
As if inhuman, insignificant
Or nonexistent.   Naturally William,
Who saw the poetry in everything,
Perceived the poetic aspect of this —
Particularly after coming back from
London, where the bewildering urban
Alienation and estrangement
Had already long since taken hold.
Awed have I been by strolling Bedlamites,
He writes in Book XII of *The Prelude,*
Referring to the road-wandering not-
Quite-normals of that not-so-remote epoch,
From many other uncouth Vagrants pass'd
In fear, have walk'd with quicker step; but why
Take note of this?   When I began to inquire,
To watch and question those I met, and held
Familiar talk with them, the lonely roads
Were school to me in which I daily read
With most delight the passions of mankind,
There saw into the depth of human souls,
Souls that appear to have no depth at all
To vulgar eyes.   I like that.   To me it feels
More considerate toward the Bedlamites
Than the shrieking street partygoers
To the street people trying to sleep this night
Of victory through, unnoticing.   It's
Their right, one might almost say, acknowledging

In the same breath that they have no rights.
Who needs a loud victory party
When all you want to do is lay your body
Down in a shop doorway, wrap your thin fleece sack
Around you, and chase a few winks. Morning
Wake-up on the street comes at five — with the light,
Now that Standard Time's back, and the clatter
And roar of garbage trucks and street cleaners.

"I have to get out of my negative
Comfort zone," Angelica's wise cousin
Peter Heinegg, Ph. D., joked
Ahead of the election, anticipating
A liberal landslide that would leave
Him little content for further volumes
Of social criticism. His *That Does It:*
Desperate Reflections on American
Culture comes with the dedication
"For Angelica — I had to dash off a
Few more jeremiads before Obama
Comes and drags me out of my negative
Comfort zone." This reminded me of a work
Whose title has always strangely intrigued
Me: Granville Hicks' *I Like America.*
My tattered paperback copy cost
Fifty cents in 1938. *"A native*
Sees his country as it is and as
It might be," the subtitle goes. And it's not
Just a rose-colored-spectacle gloss
Of a book: *Nobody Starves — Much —* perhaps
The chapter most pertinent to the scenes
I see on the streets as each night I pass

By — discusses such uncomfortable
Subjects as that phenomenon thought
Of, as recently as the Eighties,
As pure anachronism: the American
Street beggar. *Enough for Everybody*
Is another chapter. And *The Freeing
Of America.* And *Can We Work
Together?* But even with bread lines still fresh
And vivid in his mind, Hicks remains
Able to build his vision upon an America
Of known and knowable communities
That no longer exists in the world of lies
The no less honest or idealistic
Peter Heinegg needs must begin from.

Her other cousin Paul sent us a picture of
His wife Rita, a black woman, and himself,
Embracing Barack Obama, smiles all
Around. Paul had signed up fifteen hundred
Voters for the cause. Gentle line of second
Generation Americans, the Heineggs.
Paul like Peter with his brood of bright kids: So
That now, as another cousin puts it, this clan
Of transplanted Austrians has a new branch:
The Black Heineggs, citizens of the New
World that this morning has its dawn. What
I mean, O Friend! is, please don't take my lines
To mean I'm tempted to sell the New World short.

On campus the night is again cool, dark, and
Almost empty under the dripping canopy of tall
Eucalypti by the Genetics labs. *Junior,*

In which a character portrayed by
The present governor of California
Is seen to become "with child", somewhat
Like Mary toward Bethlehem to wend —
Only it's not immaculate conception
But expert science by brainy Emma
Thompson that works the supra-natural
Magic — had these labs as its fictional
Location. Well do I recall the ten long
Widebody movie production trucks
Lined up like supersized camels of
Hollywood Magi, as far as the parking
Kiosk. Not even UCLA Boosters,
When Bears host Bruins, boast that big
A bus fleet. A world is going on and constantly
Changing, changing. The Election Night
Sea of celebrants has ebbed. Away
From the crowds of tooting screaming white
People on Shattuck, five young blacks loiter
In the shadow of the labs. Four males and a
Girl. Smoking and quietly larking.
The biggest dude — athletic, in a STRIKE
FORCE windbreaker — talks quietly on cell.
The girl reels between them, singing softly
"He loves *you*," and "he loves *you*," and "he loves
You" as she goes.   Each of her friends accepts
This news in turn, without any expression
I can detect. As I skulk past, not wishing
To spoil what appears the lowest-key
And best victory party of the night,
The girl, whirling, floats up to ancient *me*.
"And he loves *you*," she sings with eyes and smile
That say, I guess, *You may be surprised by
What's coming.* And I go on my way.

What Can I Say

for human being

Someones flew a plane into a building
Or did a building fly into a plane, and then
Many someones are continuing to be alive
And some too dead; yet little has been learned
And the wars continue though who
Is fighting whom cannot be said, it all feels
So confused as though the parts no longer fit,
Or was it a failure of original creation
To leave us sans the ability to speak
To one another, some kind of freak arrival
Here on earth as now sometimes seems, too late
To help ourselves, stuck as in quicksand in
A standing pool of language, thickened then with
The algae and flotsam of time
And fear, coagulating to clog
The throat; the conscience anyway never clear…

And then one hears, from inside the dark city, a voice:
So this is what happens when the enemy is at the gate...
Time passes like this for me: it was 12 o'clock
The apple was on the tree
It was 12 o'clock and a second
The apple was not on the tree
I ate the apple and still am falling
Gracefully...
All these wars we have lost have
Pointed up the contradictions of the ethos,
The ways isolated individuals within a system

Behave do not constitute the rules of the game,
The ritual sanction of the poem demands a forgetting
After one has departed the earth, but how —
How to go on now, how to unlearn the memorized phrases,
How to build sentences of such transparency
The strange accidence of those pictures of the dead
Peels away to reveal a grammar of humanness —
Life our school, knowledge of suffering our teacher?

"Maybe it's just..."

... been feeling kind of funny lately,
only about half-here...
maybe it's just me...

can't find the joke
with a microscope, can't
tell the difference

between the smoke
and the dream
and the mirrors,

the flatness
and opacity
of the real, and the false

photographic
enhancement
of the dream...

Here

To one about to leave it, how beautiful and large
And familiar — as the old saying goes
Almost like home. And yet, the *almost* sticks
In one's throat, just as one was leaving,
Why was it never better or more?   What was
The real thing one expected?   Always somewhere
Else and never here?   And where do those
Winding roads go, and what's around the next bend
And can this really be the end?

Never thought to skywalk, had doubts
That got in the way of transcending self
With its dumb momentary occupations,
Timidly and confusedly entered caves
To find the firelight on the wall dimly signifying,
Felt awkward with the ins and outs of thought,
Cheered inwardly oft for little reason,
Was shy of others, never to draw near
Yet longed for some company to be found
Down the line, can't recall now where, in the end
Hoped only one day to find feet planted firmly
On this ground, wanted only to be *here*.

The New World was designed by Vincent Katz. It was printed in Gill Sans in an edition of 500, of which 26 are lettered A-Z and signed by the author. Printed at McNaughton & Gunn, Saline, Michigan, on 100% recycled Enviro 100 Print paper.

Also published by Libellum

March 18, 2003 by Michael Lally

Arrivederci, Modernismo by Carter Ratcliff

Not Veracruz by Joanne Kyger

Revs Of The Morrow by Ed Sanders

In The Field Where Daffodils Grow by Basil King

Natural Light by Norma Cole

TRANS/VERSIONS by Tom Clark

www.vanitasmagazine.net